UNORTHODOX LEADERSHIP

A Guide for Leading Real People in Real Organizations

SHERNETTE D. GRANT, PH.D.

Published in the United States by Unorthodox Leadership Consulting & Management Services LLC.

www.unorthodoxleadership.org

Your Publisher Number For Title Management is: 1982988

ISBN: 978-0-578-71152-2 (paperback)

Library of Congress

Name: Shernette Grant, PhD.

Title: Unorthodox Leadership: A Guide for Leading Real People in Real Organizations

Includes bibliographical references

Subjects: Leadership | Leadership Development | Organizational Leadership | Organizational Development | Management | Team Leadership | Cognitive and Behavioral Complexity & Agility |

DEDICATION

To my two beautiful daughters, Taelor and Talya, who inspire me daily to be an example of the minimum they can be, I dedicate this book to you. It is my prayer that in life you both will truly understand the value and power of the great equalizer, education, and use it to find your individual God-appointed paths in life.

TABLE OF CONTENTS

ACKNOWLEDGEMENTS

M y personal and professional road in life has always been decorated with angels whose value cannot be overstated. I take this opportunity to honor the memory of the late Dr. John Pisapia (September 7, 1937- May 2, 2017), who confirmed for me the importance of leading with purpose. He was my greatest inspiration! His uncanny love of people was evident in his ability to recognize and nurture the unique attributes of those he mentored.

It was only in his passing as I listened to others rave about his impact that I learned how far his influence spans. I dare say that is the character and heart of a great leader; the ability to make those they influence feel uniquely special, cared for and challenged to rise above every obstacle on the way to attaining their best self. His effortless ability to bring out the best in those fortunate enough to cross paths with him is something I will hold dear forever.

I would also like to especially thank Dr. Nadine Wedderburn, Arthur D. and Richard B., for helping me see the possibilities in taking the steps necessary to "touch" my next level. To my parents who since birth instilled a value for education, Mommy and Daddy, (a.k.a., Brother Vanny and Sister Bev), I love you and thank you, and to my siblings who drive me crazy but keep me grounded and encouraged, thank you.

To my beautiful daughters, Taelor and Talya, for whom I strive to be the example of "woman", strength, and humility with success, I was forever changed when you gave me real reason to thrive. Richie and Coz, thank you for your unwavering love and support, you mean the world to me! To the many friends and family who directly and indirectly influence everything I do by your constant support, I am forever grateful.

MOST importantly, thank you God for never leaving me as I have come to realize that when there were only one set of footprints in the sand, they were YOURS all the time!

LEADING AND LEADERSHIP: A PRIMER

The word "leader" is often overused and mischaracterized. Quite frequently the use of the word is triggered to describe the one or ones positioned at the top, or, at the top of the many divisions that constitute what we might refer to as the organization. Regardless of the simplicity or complexity of the organization, it is never difficult to identify the one or ones we often revere as "the leader" or "leaders". The intent of this book is not to go down the rabbit hole of making clear the distinction between leader and, manager, chief executive officer, principal, president or any other from the never-ending list; as in my entire life I have never seen an ad posted in the career section of the classifieds for a position titled "Leader". Enough said!

So that I set the tone for the pages ahead, I make two formal disclaimers. First, my use of the word "leader", in some places throughout this book, is intended as an adjective, to describe *"the one," tasked with the tremendous responsibility to convince or influence others to care about,*

and participate in accomplishing the mission or vision of the unit or organization. Second, I make the disclaimer that the use of the word "organization" henceforth is intended to refer to, "the unit", "the group", "the school", "the company" or any other institution involving people where someone is formally responsible for the collective actions and productivity of a group of individuals.

Since the extant literature on leadership is bifurcated with questions about the importance of leaders and/or leadership, many who think leaders are important, do so because they believe the organization's tone, values, and aspirations start with "a leader", e.g. the principal, the chief executive, etc. There are those also who believe leadership is not really about a single leader, but about a leader agile enough to lead the collective practice among a group of people who work together, with a focus on accomplishing a shared goal. Regardless of one's conviction, leadership as a characteristic of one, or leadership as a characteristic of many facilitated by "the one", the common denominator remains the "one".

Research clearly supports varying approaches to leadership, and I would make the argument that anyone who subscribes to a single approach might find themselves in quite a few pickles along the way. I would contend therefore that it is a leader's ability to effectively use varying approaches that demonstrate a measure of leadership success. I would further argue that a barrier to producing more successful organizations is, "the leader's" inability to shift strategies in navigating the organization as needed, and more importantly, the inability to recognize when a shift is needed.

Additionally, many leaders find it difficult to actualize theories of leadership. This explains, in part, why we do not realize more uniform and consistent success from one organization to the next or even within divisions of the same organization. Make no mistake, consistently effective leadership is not an easy feat to accomplish. Regardless of which theory of leadership to which you subscribe, I declare, the theory is NOT wrong! On the contrary, it is in its practical application with real people in real environments that deficits are identified.

In transforming organizations, leaders brave enough to employ unconventional approaches to organizational growth are fueled by a way of thinking that guides their action. Emphasis is placed on the word "brave", as unfortunately in bureaucratic environments, bravery can sometimes be enemy to the unconventional. Bravery suggests that one is poised to go against the status quo, the traditional or the expected. Therefore, leaders, in extremely complex organizations must be agile enough to navigate the organization safely and effectively.

Unorthodox Leadership

It is this way of thinking that drives brave agile actions that may be contrary to the conventional or expected that I have deemed "unorthodox leadership"; and it is this "unorthodox" approach that I have proven time and time again to be successful in actualizing the theoretical. Absent an innate disposition to employing an unorthodox approach, organizations must also create safe environments for those "not so brave" to develop their capacities for bravery. This can be achieved by prioritizing and training on the exercise of the practical, in a realm where theory is given precedence. Without a test for agility or bravery as part of the application for positions of leadership, organizations have a responsibility to nurture these characteristics in leaders who, in their exercise of leadership, will help others to embrace the organization's vision and mission. The succeeding pages offer a practical outline in three overarching areas of focus to help leaders inspire REAL people in REAL organizations.

#Unorthodoxleader; #DrGInspires

PART I

❦

HONING THE ART OF MANAGING CHANGE

A necessary precursor to innovation and growth, organizations must constantly experience and undergo change. At the heart of leading change is the notion that the more valued individuals feel by virtue of their involvement in decisions related to the change, the greater the degree of cooperation and the greater the level of support the leader will realize. As such, it is imperative that leaders understand that in its most basic and practical application, leadership is not an individual sport. In his research dated back to 1991, Neumann, asserted that more effective leadership is more likely to occur when driven by a pool of administrative competencies derived from having individuals who are highly cognitive in orientation participating in the thinking process, than from a single heroic figure.

Though no one would argue that "the leader" ultimately bears the accountability for such things as; setting direction, developing staff, redesigning the organization, and managing outcomes, decades of research is clear about the added value to a more expansive, collective and collaborative approach to leadership (Gurr & Drysdale, 2013; Kythreotis et al., 2010; Leithwood, 2005). As such, no longer is the leader characterized as the primary "thinker" and "doer", but instead, as the one with the ability to harness the creative thinking of those within the organization (Evans, 2007; Kythreotis et al., 2010). This idea is prominently represented in several theories about leadership: transformative, distributive, collective and so on.

The act of making members of an organization feel valued is one a leader must consider and actively work to accomplish. Without very deliberate consideration for ensuring this happens, leaders often find themselves faced with repercussions characterized by defiance or indifference; neither of which are conducive to moving a leader's or an organization's agenda forward. Of the most popular approaches to ensuring cooperation is the act of involving members of the organization in the decision-making, and processes related to the desired outcome. This kind of involvement has the positive consequence of bringing together and acknowledging the impact of the collective thinking of a group of individuals. As such, effective leadership continues to be judged according to the creativity with which diverse skills and abilities are harnessed from the workforce to effect change and increase innovation.

There is also a growing body of research that examines

the cognitive aspects of leadership that facilitate a leader's ability to navigate the organization and make sense of multiple stimuli that drive decisions related to organizational processes (Evans, 2007; Hallinger, Leithwood, & Murphy, 1993; Pisapia, 2009; Spillane et al., 2002). Included in these decisions are those around how best to utilize individuals within the organization to drive established goals which often involve change. This sentiment is grounded in decades of study by many of the most notable experts in the field of leadership who have supported the notion that leaders poised to bring out the best in their staffs must exhibit cognitively agile and complex, thinking; both characteristics of a flexible mindset. As such, the art of managing change as the first of 3 strategies explored in this book for developing the unorthodox leader skillset is outlined in the 5 succeeding steps.

1: EMBRACE A FLEXIBLE MINDSET

Dating back to 1996, Bieri et al. formally defined cognitive complexity as one's capacity to construct social behaviors in multidimensional ways. Considered a psychological characteristic, cognitive complexity refers to the amount of "brain power" used by individuals in shaping perceptions about things they encounter or situations in which they find themselves. Individuals who exhibit high levels of cognition are deemed multidimensional in their thinking and are superior in their ability to analyze and differentiate situations or problems into many components.

They are further able to explore, make connections, and identify relationships among different components to determine a path forward (Bieri, 1966; Granello, 2010). A cognitively complex individual is communicative, adaptive by nature, exhibits flexibility in thinking, and has the capacity to respond at a moment's notice to changes in their environment (Gonzalez, 2004; LePine, Colquitt, & Erez, 2000; Massingham, 2013). It is this flexibility in thinking that makes them excellent strategic planners and drive their ability to assess and problem-solve to produce actions in support of positive outcomes.

While leaders may possess an array of skills that make them cognitively complex, exercising these skills will make them cognitively agile. Cognitive agility refers to a leader's ability to adapt and maneuver his or her complex thoughts to produce action in response to change in people, processes, organizational structures, technology and environmental influences among others (Horney et al., 2010; Pisapia, 2009). Cognitive agility as defined by the late Dr. John Pisapia (2009), famed researcher and academic, is the capability of an individual to rapidly and cost-efficiently adapt mentally to changes in their environment.

Leadership agility refers to the propensity of an individual to process information and act by using a combination of interpretive, analytical, and evaluative skills despite changes in conditions (Horney et al., 2010; Joiner & Josephs, 2007). According to McKenzie and Aitken (2012), agile leaders are able to maintain stability and consistency in an organization, regardless of how diverse or fragmented the organization is. An agile leader is also able to manage organizational climate by negotiating conflicting personalities and groups of individuals within the organization (Horney et al., 2010; McKenzie & Aitken, 2012).

Agility, therefore, is a key characteristic of a leader who is adept at adjusting to and managing change. This is especially true in the context of the broader group or environment where it becomes necessary to interpret events that take place from a variety of different perspectives while at the same time reacting to multiple stimuli and making sense of what is going on in the surrounding environment (Horney et al., 2010; Weick, 1995).

The ability to see "the big picture," have a deep and thoughtful understanding of how components of systems interrelate and work together and understanding the impact that internal and external factors have on the overall successful operation of systems is key (Lewis et al., 2014; Pisapia, 2009). Leaders who exhibit this kind of versatility in thinking, characterized by the ability to recognize the interdependence between numerous elements while exercising coherence in decision-making, can successfully improve organizational performance and sustain positive change. This characteristic has been widely tied to leader effectiveness (Pisapia, 2009).

In combat, agility is typified by robustness, resilience, responsiveness, flexibility, innovativeness, and adaptability (Thornton, 2005). Agility represents a cognitive domain and, as in war, is a necessary trait that allow leaders to not only conceptualize what needs to be done, but through execution and action, do what needs to be done (Thornton, 2005). In a study conducted by the Institute for Corporate Productivity (2010), a measure of agility involving over 400 leaders targeted their ability to anticipate and initiate change, as well as recognize and respond to challenges effectively and efficiently. Studies of this nature underscore that it is not enough for leaders to simply manage change, but it is also important that they are able to embrace the advantages that change brings while operating in a mode where anticipation of change is commonplace (Institute for Corporate Productivity, 2010). Organizations that have been shown to embrace the value of agility in leadership have also proven to be more successful than those that do not (Horney et al., 2010).

Though the need to problem-solve and exercise deductive reasoning is not exclusive to leaders (indeed, it is a requirement of human existence), it is the degree to which each individual exercises these skills that provides a barometer by which human thinking and actions are set apart. It is difficult to argue with the idea that the degree to which good decision-making skills are exercised by human beings is one criterion by which one may be elevated to the role of "leader". Granello and Underfer-Babalis (2004) found that individuals with high levels of cognition utilize information and perceive it in flexible and strategic manners, while those with low cognition have fixed perceptions, which in turn results in the exercise of a fixed set of actions. The latter has no place in the dynamic and changing environments that characterize 21st century organizations where the need to problem-solve, and lead change and innovation, is dependent on the exercise of dynamic skills.

Despite this however, and with the understanding that even in leadership there are varying degrees and levels of cognition, the need to grow leaders in this area of cognition is key. It is incumbent on leaders, and the leaders of leaders to address this need with a more thoughtful and direct approach, by providing actionable guidance on how leaders might grow in their exercise of cognition. In doing so, the ability to cultivate and grow leaders in the skills necessary to pull together teams to lead and manage change becomes a reality, especially in difficult and dynamic environments. These skills will allow leaders to carry out their main responsibility; that of leading REAL PEOPLE in REAL ORGANIZATIONS.

In all arenas, cognitively complex and agile leaders must navigate similarly complex environments. The leader's role, that of thinking by considering multiple perspectives with consideration for the broader group of individuals requires an even more complex mode of operation (Del Favero, 2006). Leaders in these settings must be able to interpret events that take place in the organization from a variety of different perspectives, make sense of what is going on around them, and have the ability to lead in that respect (Anderson, 1983; Weick, 1995). The need for increasingly agile leaders who can think in these complex ways become even more critical.

With the understanding that great leaders exercise superior thinking skills, one is inclined to ask, how then might these skills be used to influence those they lead to *"care about, and participate in accomplishing the mission or vision of the unit or organization?"* In its practical application, a leader must be able to develop and nurture healthy, cooperative and productive work relationships. They must exemplify the art of working closely with superiors, colleagues, and those they supervise, to lead in a manner that encourages relationship-building and productivity. Leaders who operate from this perspective are cognizant of the needs of their workers but are adept at balancing productivity with personal needs (Granello & Underfer-Babalis, 2004). A leader who embraces this mindset is well on their way to success!

2: STEP BACK TO MOVE FORWARD

To garner support from individuals in an organization, the leader must invest the time and effort to study and understand the norms and values of the organization where they operate. Take note, this is not the equivalent of agreeing to, or conforming to existing organizational values or norms.

They must however understand and value the power of said norms and values, as one should never underestimate the influence that traditional practices have in individuals' response, resistance and outlook on change. How often as a leader have you heard the phrase "We never did it this way?" Enough said! These norms and values, especially if they do not align to the new vision, must be considered and tackled as a precursor to achieving a desired action and or mindset change.

It is also imperative that, as the current leader, you are aware of and understand the approaches of previous leaders and the values and norms they previously established that are still pervasive within the organization. You must scope out past leadership practices as any attempt to make changes to those practices without pre-work is almost guaranteed to be met with varying degrees of opposition. This is especially true if the previous leader was held in high regards by an overwhelming majority of the individuals in the organization.

Be warned and check your mindset at the door when dealing with opposition. Accept the realization that this challenge will come, and it is simply a matter of when and how adamantly it comes across, NOT if. Though as leaders, we cannot prepare for ALL things that will come our way, preparing to respond to the change-averse challenges means consciously thinking about it, and processing why the new direction is the right one for the organization. Be reminded that human nature will instinctively interpret any suggestion of change as your unspoken declaration that something is being done wrong and consequently, as your attack on the "past". It is for this reason that you must take great care to constantly verbalize that there are no comparisons being established. Remind the team often of how grateful you are for the work that has been done in the past to position you to lead them in building on past practices and accomplishments, to grow the organization and evolve with the times. I will also caution at this point that you should be prepared to restate this reminder many, many, many, many, times as years of experience have taught me that a consequence of change-averseness is willful forgetfulness, which is also deleterious to the overall health of the organization.

Be reminded, embracing the historical context of the organization does not equate to conforming to current or past practices. The intent of this action is to demonstrate a posture of preparedness to tackle opposition as a result of individual members' loyalty to past values, norms and practices. Embracing and honoring the past is among the main keys to unlocking the path to a successful future.

3: GET TO KNOW THE PEOPLE

Leader actions in forging authentic relationships are key considerations for creating healthy and dynamic environments. Much like the body is dependent on the interconnectedness and collective functioning of the nervous, respiratory, and other systems, organizations comprised of individuals who truly work together, instead of against each other, are healthier and more productive. This is at the heart of building relationships and getting to know members of the organization.

In getting to know individuals within the organization, the leader's responsibility is to consider "the people" as a combination of an individuals' personal and professional attributes. It is this true understanding of the unique attributes of individual members that will drive decisions about their role in moving the organization's vision or mission along. Since leaders lead people and not things, it is imperative that as a leader, you are connected to the implications individuals' personal or professional attributes have on harming or helping the work. Armed with that awareness, have a plan to mitigate or harness!

The goal of getting to know your pool of personnel competence is to consider how and where everyone will be included in the master plan as part of a team committed or influenced to make the organizational goals their priority. The work of each member of the organization will look different, but if we consider the organization a team, then each team member's role is equally important! The ability to harness the contributions of each team member while having a plan to mitigate destructive practices will produce constructive outcomes, enhance the creative process and increase efficiencies. A leader's ability to leverage the collective power of the team by relying on the pooled intelligence of its members, is essential to moving organizations in the right direction. This does not require a hierarchical approach, but instead, the creation of a community of practice characterized by trust, professionalism and humility, and where leadership occurs in a very organic manner through involvement of others.

Make no mistake, it remains the leader's responsibility to ensure enabling and supportive environments within which the team operates. However, the role of the leader must evolve from the one who does the job to the one who supports in the role of facilitator to get the job done. A supportive leader also facilitates cohesion among team members. Additionally, since the level of performance and satisfaction accomplished by the team is based on the skillset of the people involved, the leader also has the responsibility to remove obstacles, and if necessary, remove members who negatively impact the team's work (Gerras & Clark, 2011).

To appropriately assign and support each member of the team, it is imperative to get to know them individually. In doing so, the leader is also able to determine the level and type of support needed by each member. It also becomes necessary that the leader and facilitator of the group is able to differentiate among those on the team able to operate autonomously from those needing to be monitored. Know who to empower for autonomous functioning and who to monitor for support! Taking the time to get to know members of the organization or unit is an investment in future successes. Knowing what each member brings or can bring to the team is imperative to harnessing personnel resources for the benefit of attaining organizational goals. Make it a priority!

It is also imperative that leaders pay close attention to staff members' motives. Explore motives and intentions with a respectful, honest and sincere attitude. In doing so, you will gain better insight on the oppositional forces as you think through your approach with that group of individuals. I profess that the old adage "keep your friends close and your enemies closer" is true also in leadership. Be intuitive and hone your ability to look beyond the surface.

In getting to know the opposition, do not remain fixated on their approach, but adjust expeditiously to strategies for intercepting disruptive attempts. Engage them through deliberate involvement in decision-making and public delivery of new information. In many instances, your opponents will need to become champions of your cause! Remain cautious however in using this strategy and know when to "move on" as giving attention to negative behaviors in some instances can breed more negative behaviors. With that said, DO NOT neglect individuals who are moving in the right direction; and be sure to praise and reward openly! As you get to know team members, you are better able to make educated decisions about their place and role in the organization!

Be cognizant also that subordinates are instinctively and, in most cases, initially on their best behavior. This may especially be the case when a new supervisor comes on board. Do not confuse behaviors with intent or ability. There will be those whose immediate goal and target is to secure the favor and approval of their new leader, or to use socially driven interactive tactics to deter and discourage deeper scrutiny. Be unapologetically inquisitive about the work and leave no stone unturned but master the art of being warm, inviting, personable, but non-committal. Hone your skills for deep and pervasive questioning; be observant; learn to dig deep; and be slow to agree, co-sign or make judgement calls!

Finally, be sure to check your expectations at the door. Understand the hand you have been dealt and embrace the notion that the people do not influence your change plan, but instead, your change plan influences the people. Stick to the plan, keep expectations high for yourself and your team members, and embrace your responsibility to make them believers!

4: SET UP THE PLAY

In the paragraphs ahead, I utilize a sports analogy to emphasize an important leader action in managing change. It is imperative that leaders understand that planning for change begins with setting up the play ahead of disclosing the game plan, and in fact prior to unveiling any specific details of the upcoming game. Planning for change therefore begins way before a specific project is on the table for discussion.

I had previously mentioned how averse the average human being is to change and as such, leader success is directly tied to a leader's ability to help members of the team overcome this fear and become comfortable with the general concept of "change." In setting up the play, begin with executing several subtle projects. Make rudimentary and superficial changes that, in the big scheme of things, may have minimal impact but boost morale. Examples of such things include, beautification projects, changing aesthetics, changes to work schedules, re-organizing spaces and moving people around. Guaranteed to cause discomfort and uneasiness, these things at their core do not change the fundamental vision or mission of the organization and are difficult to oppose. This discomfort is what you seek, so maintain your game face and be patient. Create the initial discomfort of the "unknown" or the "what next" while at the same time subliminally establishing that change is harmless.

Be sure to take great care in this phase to include projects and items that have the potential to add value to individuals' outlook. Include things that have great potential to help individuals feel good about themselves and the organization within which they exist. An example of such a project could involve orchestrating a make-over to the lunchroom or a common space that individuals share and enjoy. Though insignificant in the big scheme of things, be sure to make these changes observable to the broader environment or community. In doing so, you are creating wins that pull the entire community closer together.

It is through these subtle wins that you will garner support when the real game begins. As you go through this phase, speak often about the potential work ahead and create excitement without divulging specifics. Be sure to validate the team by reminding them of your dependence on the value and expertise you anticipate they will be contributing to future work ahead. Set the stage for individuals to understand that it is simply a matter of when, NOT if, the change will come.

It is in this phase of the plan that one is establishing that change is inevitable and the subtle opportunities for practice is merely a way of removing or decreasing the tensions and fear of the unknown. Helping team members achieve a healthy level of comfort with change reflective of the dynamic nature of a 21st century environment is key.

5: BUILD A FAN BASE

Needless to say, leaders are ultimately held accountable for ensuring acceptable levels of organizational performance. Although research has identified contradictions in factors of influence by leaders, many studies identify the positive relationship between leader quality and the overall conditions in the organization.

I pause here to offer my own interpretation and analogy of the widely purported difference between leadership and management. At the risk of generalizing, management practices are focused on what I describe as the "tangibles", i.e. operational items tied directly to profits, test scores, productivity and products. Leadership practices on the other hand emphasizes what I call the "intangibles", for example, motivation and enthusiasm as intrinsic attributes of people. The basic premise is that, if "people" are performing at their highest, because they are motivated and enthusiastic, the "tangibles" will increase or be improved. Certainly, one should not exist without the other, but noteworthy is the observable direct link between the "people" and the "products."

To impact "product," leaders must therefore influence people. What comes through in this analogy is the notion that leader influence is indirectly related to the outcomes by way of their impact on the people. In essence, leaders influence people to be their best and, in turn, people give of their best! This indirect link between leader and product is why it is crucially important for leaders to think through their actions relative to people, as missteps can have lasting and damaging impact on people's motivation or enthusiasm to produce.

The preceding analogy points to the value attached to, and the significance of treating people well. It is important to support members of the team by celebrating personal milestones such as birthdays and accomplishments. It is imperative that as a leader you become a listener. Listen and lend support for personal and professional concerns. Empathize and provide support. Mentor, counsel and coach as this not only builds trust around your leadership, but it also grows those you lead.

This is also the time it becomes even more important than ever to establish that willingness to get in the game and play alongside members of the team. Getting in the game alongside the players in the organization has tremendous potential to encourage trust and commitment. As a leader, if you have never heard the words "I will do it just for you" from members of your team, reconsider your approach and take a critical look at your fan base or lack thereof. Winning the affection of team members will prove useful in garnering support for future projects because, when people feel valued and are treated well by their superiors, more often than not they reciprocate!

PART II

ॐ

HONING THE ART OF MANAGING TEAMS

The use of teams in leading organizational growth or facilitating organizational practices as an extension of "the leader" has increasingly become a focal point in organizational effectiveness (Parris & Vickers, 2005). The team approach to leadership embraces collaboration among different constituencies in an organization, emphasizes the idea of shared power and expertise, and enables such functions as organizational planning and goal setting to benefit from creativity and efficacy as a result of collective effort (Gurr & Drysdale, 2013; Leithwood, 2005; Leithwood & Mascall, 2008; McLean, 2013). Additionally, this collective approach to leadership allows for the distribution of labor and the ability to tap into individuals' varied talents and skills. It produces interdependence among individuals and an appreciation for how individual actions and behaviors impact the whole (Leithwood & Mascall, 2008). Especially true of complex societies characterized by economic and social interrelationships, teams that produce positive performance outcomes are more successful in their ability to share in the exchange of ideas and learn from each other.

As such, teams have cemented their place as an important component of modern-day and high performing organizations (Burke et al., 2006; Day, Gronn, & Salas, 2004; Wendt, Euwema, & van Emmerik, 2009, Katzenback & Smith, 1993b). A team is defined as a specific group of people who have complementary skills, and are committed to a clear and common purpose or a set of performance goals, and has been assigned specific authority to manage and lead a process while holding themselves mutually accountable for specified outcomes (Hackman, 2002; Katzenbach & Smith, 1993a; Katzenbach & Smith, 1993b).

Much of the research on team leadership has focused on leadership as an input factor; that is, leadership brought to a team by virtue of the actions of an individual in leading the team (Day et al., 2004). Team leadership should be examined from the perspective of leadership outcomes that can be generated when individuals work together and are led by a savvy and agile leader to accomplish shared tasks (Day et al., 2004; O'Connor & Quinn, 2004). Leadership therefore should not be focused on the actions of any one person, but on the collective result of the actions of all team members.

With the understanding that successful teams require individuals to utilize skills necessary for building good working relationships while keeping organizational goals at the forefront, Barnard (2005) submitted that individuals as part of a leadership structure must undergo specific training to ensure that team members are able to communicate, solve problems, and manage complex situations. Despite the potential greatness that can be accomplished through the work of teams however, they often do not reach their full potential. In fact, according to Barnett and McCormick (2012), many teams fail to realize their goals. This elicits the question, why? Earlier in this book, we explored some key areas where leader influence and actions are key to successful outcomes, and this area of leading teams is no exception.

Pisapia's (2009) claim that successful leaders think with the end in mind is of significant relevance here. In looking ahead to the end, leaders must be able to exercise a series of step-by-step strategic thinking skills in shaping ideas for outcomes. Although members of most teams typically do not undergo any form of training to enhance their abilities to coalesce and think in ways Pisapia suggested, the expectation is that teams are able to effectively function and be productive as a unit.

For teams to lead with success, it is crucial that together as a unit they exhibit characteristics common to leaders. Great leadership is key to encouraging team members to value the ideas of others within the group and pay close attention to ideas presented by others. Through mental stimulation, this sharing of ideas has also been shown to increase cognition (Nijstad & Stroebe, 2006). Leaders therefore bear the responsibility to guide and lead the cultivation of these characteristics among team members. The 2 subsequent steps provide a guide for leaders to do so effectively.

6: BUILD THE TEAM

Since teams are usually assembled to accomplish or lead a task or variety of tasks, it is imperative that team members be chosen based on skill sets and their ability to learn new skills. No team will be successful if there aren't individuals on the team capable of exercising skills conducive to task completion (Katzenback & Smith, 1993a).

Many attempts have been made to study the science of teaming to develop a model for identifying strategies most appropriate for encouraging effective collaboration (Falk-Krzesinski et al., 2011; Stokols et al., 2008). Studies with this focus show that although the effectiveness of teaming is highly dependent on the setting, it is also dependent on the readiness of its members to collaborate through the exercise of flexible, inclusive and cooperative actions (Stokols et al., 2008).

Team members must understand the value of group processes such as conflict resolution, negotiation, discussions, agreements, and disagreements in cultivating productive dialogue to achieve consensus (Boni et al., 2009; Israel et al., 1998). A leader's ability to cultivate these attributes in team members has been shown to produce more cohesive teams as a precursor to generating productive and effective outcomes. It also becomes necessary to consider individual personalities, team structures and the reciprocal relationship between the team and the organization as contributing factors to overall cohesiveness (Wendt et al., 2009). In considering personalities, think about how they will govern and work together, as it is never acceptable to believe you can harness the professional potentials of individuals without consideration for the personal!

Leaders who involve the broader group in leading the organization have been shown to be more successful. To increase the probability for success, leaders should be purposeful in building the team to lead. Being thoughtful about the team selection process enhances the chance that not only the right people will be selected, but that once selected, the right people are assigned to the right roles and the right tasks. This however does not assume that all members of the team will perform at the same level, but such is the reality of building teams in real organizations with real people. Therein lies the work of a leader – getting each team member to recognize and maximize their potential!

Leaders should therefore take great care in assigning team members to positions on the team that will bring the most value to the work of the team and to the organization. Be reminded, this is among the many reasons it is critically important to get to know the members of the organization. It is this knowledge that will guide the process of building smaller and more focused groups to accomplish the work. In strategically placing individuals, utilize your cognitively more advanced team members as quasi-leaders within the group. Recognize who your leaders and early adaptors are, and coach, nurture and empower them. On the contrary, identify your "lagers" and think strategically about how you will encourage participation and cooperation. Placing "lagers" in a place of influence could accelerate this process. Be cautious, however, and establish boundaries early when exercising this strategy.

Be sure also to include members of the organization who are guaranteed to represent the opposition, either due to deficits in their own performance or by virtue of their rebellious spirit. I would argue that in many instances "we" (adults) exhibit some of the same tendencies we often identify and criticize in children. We mask or distract when the spotlight is placed on our insecurities, or in some cases, we simply activate our fighting spirits. Be sure however to think through your plan to monitor and establish boundaries for those with the natural affinity to disrupt. Become the best lemonade maker in the organization!

Identify your moles and strategically utilize them. A mole in this context is not intended to align with the notion of violation of trust or betrayal but, instead, are early adaptors from the wider group who are among the most trusted and respected by the masses. This group of early adaptors will become extremely useful in bringing others along. They become the mouthpieces for the message. Be reminded, almost every message coming from the leader for noncooperative individuals will be met with scrutiny. Advance your vision by utilizing individuals within the organization who are trusted and held in high regard. Your goal is to win for the organization and win for the people you serve, so empower others to help you do so and allow them to take credit for the outcomes you have authored!

7: SUPPORT THE TEAM

Leaders should always embrace a posture of parenting. Parents foster, support and promote the physical, social-emotional and intellectual wellbeing of children. Great parents celebrate their children. Great parents hold their children accountable for good behavior and expect them to achieve at their highest. Great parents correct and instruct at the risk of being momentarily "unpopular" or "unloved". Great parents often must wait for children to grow up to be appreciated for the accountability standards they enforced. Great parents are quick to praise and slow to criticize. Great parents are forgiving. Great parents do not parent to be recognized. Great parents gladly make sacrifices for their children. Great parents communicate expectations often, and great parents constantly coach and provide guidance for emotional and intellectual development.

In supporting your team, the best way to build trust and cooperation is to parent! Communicating and exercising effective feedback practices can greatly improve performance (Kayes, Kayes, & Kolb, 2005). Not only does communication promote the exchange of information relevant to the team's work and the organization as a whole, but it is also a great way to build trust and promote a culture of psychological safety among team members (Edmonson, 1999; Granello & Underfer-Babalis, 2004). This level of trust is essential to positive interaction, promoting collaboration, and in building relationships (Derek, Morfitt, & Demaerschalk, 1996).

Understand that any attempt at supporting your team is intimately connected to their openness to being supported. As such, this is highly dependent on team members' perception of you as the leader. Your ability to support will therefore be dependent on how transparent, relatable, humble, humane, vulnerable, and genuine you are perceived. In demonstrating these traits, share personal stories, good and bad, so that your team can see you as a 'real person' dealing with the same issues they do in everyday life. Be empathetic and do not berate.

Let us dig deeper into the role that accountability plays in supporting team members. Understand that great leaders balance accountability with compassion. It is imperative that you establish the expectations for getting the work done despite personal challenges. Support your employees as much as is reasonable but know when to make the switch from support to correction or, in some cases, discipline. Know when to remove individuals from the team and know when to make substitutions when the actions of an individual or group of individuals are counterproductive to the work of the group. In doing so, however, always do so with respect and ALWAYS allow individuals to walk away with their dignity intact.

Holding individuals accountable is also one way of supporting the team and the organization. Be cautioned however, that often, accountability measures will be met with aggressive stances. In these cases, be fair, be consistent, and ignore the pouting on the sidelines from disgruntled team members who have been "benched". That will pass. Give minimal energy to this kind of behavior and move on to support the priorities of the team. In many instances, if the foundation was previously laid as it relates to the relationship between the individual and the leader, aggression is temporary; as the leader would have already established a genuine posture of care and high expectations. Ultimately, the leader will emerge on the other side of grace, just as a parent would. As a leader, the moment you can reprimand an employee and the conversation ends with a hug is the moment you know, healthy relationships were fostered!

It is also imperative that in this space, the leader is forgiving and DOES NOT hold grudges. If individuals feel that they have been harmed by past experiences or cannot see the benefit of being involved with the team, the likelihood of future success in working together will be greatly diminished (Israel et al., 1998). Members of the organization should also be able to express disagreements respectfully without concern for retaliatory or lingering consequences. Embrace future opportunities to enable individuals to regain their confidence to re-commit and re-engage in the work when appropriate by placing them back in the game providing they have something valuable to contribute.

As you support the work of your team, find balance between listening to constant complaining and knowing when to stop. Be savvy at identifying when no solution is ever a solution but is instead just an opening to a new complaint. In managing complaining, know when to stop entertaining "the complaining" and help employees in transition to a solutions-oriented posture by insisting that every complaint be accompanied by a suggestion for potential solution. Again, perform these actions with respect and always allow employees to walk away from any of these conversations with their dignity intact.

The extent to which individuals want to remain a part of a team is a good indication of how satisfied they are in their roles, as well as how valued they feel as part of the team (Organ, Podsakoff, & MacKenzie, 2006; Schermerhorn et al., 2002). When members of teams feel socially connected to each other or are committed to the accomplishment of a task or attainment of a common goal, team functioning is greatly enhanced.

This argument assumes that despite the role of the team as a unit of leadership, organizations also possess a single figurehead, the leader whose actions are key to this process. Leading with this level of authenticity helps individuals develop a sense of commitment to the organization. As a result, team members, through their collective habits and actions, cultivate a climate of integrity, respect, and trust, which in turn encourages a positive outlook about the team and the organization (Boni et al., 2009; Cameron, Bright, & Caza, 2004).

PART III

c∕∕∕∕∕∕∕∕∕∕∕∕∕∕∕∕

HONING THE ART OF EXECUTION

A leader's ability to transform and or move his/her organization from point A to point B is crucial to the success of the organization (Pisapia, 2009). In getting to point B, a successful leader must be able to visualize and strategize steps needed to get to that point. The right balance between visioning and doing is crucial to successful leadership; it is in the doing that the work is evidenced (Pisapia, 2009). Pisapia (2009) and Kotter (1996) both discussed the idea that vision without strategy is useless. According to Kotter (1996), "A vision can be mundane and simple, at least partially, because in successful transformations it is only one element in a larger system that also includes strategies and plans..." (p. 71).

Effectiveness in leadership has long been tied to a leader's ability to exercise a wide repertoire of skills in leading initiatives to meet the needs of their organizations (Lawrence, Lenk, & Quinn, 2009; Tsui, 1984). Research has shown that a leader's ability to vary and differentiate his or her behaviors and actions, and adjust as necessary to meet the dynamic needs of the organization while managing the personalities within, is more successful than their counterparts who do not possess these skills (Hooijberg, 1996; Williams, 1994).

This repertoire of skills requires that the leader can exhibit diverse yet complementary behaviors that allow them to respond appropriately to the myriad of scenarios they encounter in their roles (Hooijberg, Hunt, & Dodge, 1997; Lawrence et al., 2009; Zaccaro, 2001). Not only does this aid in task accomplishment but it is also key to managing personalities and situations. The dichotomy of conflicting behaviors and actions insists that at their core, leaders must be flexible. This attribute of flexibility is reflected in what research describes as being the behaviorally complex leader (Denison, Hooijberg, & Quinn, 1995).

Behaviorally complex leaders are multi-directional in their approach and have documented far more successful outcomes compared to their counterparts who are not. Behavioral complexity deals with the idea that some leaders possess a reservoir of skills that they are able to use depending on the situation, and precludes the idea that while the leader possesses said skills, it is the exercise of those skills that makes the leader behaviorally agile (Hooijberg, 1996). Agility, simply defined, is the ability to change direction quickly (Bloomfield, Ackland, & Elliot, 1994). Considering the dynamism of the 21st century organization, a leader must be able to respond to changes in the organization at a moment's notice. It is in the exercise of change-impacting actions that behavioral agility is evidenced.

In sports, the term agility has been used to describe the physical body's change in movement in response to a stimulus. Further, it is associated with an individual's adaptability to the dynamics of the physical setting while acknowledging the individual's ability to utilize cognitive skills, such as visual-scanning and anticipation (Sheppard & Young, 2006). Recent research has focused on improving the ability of sprinters to anticipate and achieve effective body positioning as a means of eliciting optimal performance when they must change directions on the track (Sheppard & Young, 2006). A leader's ability to identify the need for, and utilize the appropriate or a combination of, certain key leadership actions makes that leader behaviorally agile.

Through a leader's ability to sense the needs of the organization and its people, behaviorally agile leaders can adjust their behaviors to suit the needs of the group they serve (Hooijberg, 1996). According to Pisapia (2009), one of the most basic functions of an effective leader is the ability to identify a specified goal, determine the direction the organization will take, and put into action a plan that will facilitate transformation of the organization. The ability to adapt and respond appropriately to the complexities of one's environment and be multi-dimensional in the approach to problem solving and managing relationships is also key (Ernst, 2000; Hooijberg & Quinn, 1992).

In a dynamic and changing environment, a behaviorally complex individual can handle paradox and contradiction by not only exercising a variety of leadership functions, but also by determining which functions to utilize and when (Hooijberg, 1996). Behavioral complexity is situational in nature; hence, individuals who are behaviorally complex can modify their actions and utilize multiple responses in addressing organizational and environmental needs (Ernst, 2000). This kind of behavior becomes the breeding ground for agility. Agile leaders therefore respond to organizational needs with focused, fast, and flexible actions (Horney et al., 2010).

Pisapia (2009) contended that behavioral skills evidenced through leader-influenced actions are necessary to effect change or sustain organizational growth. Executing the right balance in employing these actions will lead to highly skilled and effective leaders, as the complex and agile nature of these actions mirror the cognitive domain within which a leader must exist. As such, the more complex and agile a leader's behaviors are, the more likely they are to realize the goals and vision of their organization. In an article published by the Balanced Scorecard Report (Kaplan, Norton, & Barrow, 2008), the idea of strategy development following the creation of a vision for a company is discussed as necessary in creating a sustainable advantage. In fact, vision is discussed as only the first step in strategy development (Kaplan et al., 2008).

Whether leadership as a construct of "the one" or a construct of "the one leading the group", behaviorally agile and complex skills are necessary to executing. Though setting clear and focused goals in line with an organization's vision and mission are necessary to improve the collective efforts of any team, it is through the collective actions of its members that actionable outcomes will be realized (Gerras & Clark, 2011; Katzenback & Smith, 1993a; Ogilvie & Jelavic, 2009; Stokols et al., 2008). The use of behaviors that focus on task accomplishment as well as people management are key to effective outcomes. With the knowledge that task accomplishment is the ultimate reason for which teams are assembled, the individual or collective actions of members of the team precipitate task completion. The extent to which teams have been successful in accomplishing tasks have been tied directly to how the team is led.

Now that we understand the role leader mindset and leader influence play in organizational growth, let us consider how this translates to actionable items, outlined in the following step.

8: EXECUTE WITH CONFIDENCE

Now that you have prepared yours and the mindset of the people you serve, as well as built a functioning and cooperative coalition around any work ahead, the next step is to get the work done. It's time to make the pitch! Beware, however, that though you have set the stage for your work ahead, this is not the time to "take over." Be reminded, leadership is still a team sport. More now than ever, this is the time to engage the team in the "doing." A good strategy for kicking this off is to begin by posing a question intended to solicit thinking around the problem to be solved or get individuals thinking about how an issue or process may be resolved or enhanced. Question...DON'T tell! Allow the team through your guiding to arrive at the realization that there is work to be done. Once you have engaged the team in identifying the work and the reason for the work, further engage them in developing a plan for addressing and identifying the role they each will play in executing the plan.

Your role as the leader remains to make it safe for team members to think big. Push the thinking of the group to encourage innovation and re-imagining. Challenge their thinking and learn to guide graciously. Utilize and engage your formal and informal leaders, as well as your moles in this process. As you work through the execution phase, hone the skill of allowing others to take credit for your ideas. However, do not relinquish or abandon your vision; unless, of course, a member of the team presents a better one. Yes, "the leader" is not the only member of the team that can contribute to vision. In fact, visioning is also intended to be a team sport. Be prepared to adjust the game plan as input is received and be sure to give credit where it is due. This is a great strategy for encouraging participation. The important thing to remember or consider is that the ultimate goal is task accomplishment, and as you already know, there are many ways that goals can be accomplished. Utilize the team to arrive at and embrace the best path but, as the leader, know the end game before stepping into the negotiating room!

In delivering on a mission know when to push and know when to pull back. Know when to cuddle and when to provide tough love. Most importantly, embrace your role as the highest paid sales executive in the organization…become good, no, become GREAT at it!

CONCLUSION

❧

In response to the ongoing need for organizations to reinvent themselves and grow in response to environmental variables, many strategies and approaches have been deployed over the years. One such approach that continues to gain popularity is that of placing value on leadership as a catalyst for growth. The literature clearly points to the role of effective leaders in promoting positive change and improving organizational outcomes. Leaders capable of exerting influence through the building of positive relationships that enhance a sense of connectivity among individuals and to the organization, wins!

Leader actions that encourage the feeling of personal responsibility for outcomes, positive or negative, is key to accelerating organizational growth (Sutton & Rao, 2014). When accountability is accelerated, leaders can be confident that they are achieving important milestones and the organization is moving in the right direction.

Although there is extensive research in support of individual leadership, there is also a growing body of research in support of team leadership that relies on the collaborative and collective coalescing of several individuals represented as a team. Regardless of one's conviction as to whether leadership is a characteristic of an individual or a team, research is explicit about specific prevalent characteristics necessary for successful leadership. A leader's ability to harness the collective power and synergy of a collaborating group of individuals is key (Gerras & Clark, 2011). Leader influence is crucial to encouraging innovative thinking as an accelerant for organizational change and growth.

Research on organizational health and productivity identifies a dependence on a leader's intentional approach to improving the organization (Gulsen & Gulenay, 2014; MacNeil, Prater, & Busch, 2009). In perfecting the art of managing change, leaders who actively think about how to make this happen will likely increase their chances for success. For some, this comes naturally and happens organically, but for others, they must work actively at it. Whether it comes naturally or not, the preceding chapters outlined some very practical steps that leaders can employ as necessary for growing an organization and facilitating innovation.

Research and personal experience confirm that teams are also an integral part of organizational structures. If the leadership provided by these teams contributes in a meaningful manner to the overall success of the organizations, then a reasonable assumption is that team members should collectively exhibit characteristics commonly identified in successful leaders. For teams to identify with the use of effective strategy for leadership, they must be guided by leaders capable of providing the level of support necessary to cultivate effective skills or habits. Make no mistake, the need for support is not a measure of strength or weakness of the team, and neither is it an excuse for encouraging mediocrity. On the contrary, it is a necessary leader action, as a leader who is supportive of his or her team is laser-focused on support for maintaining high expectations as a precursor to enhanced team performance and improved organizational outcomes.

Ultimately, every organization exists for a specified purpose. It is in accomplishing or exceeding said purpose that the organization's effectiveness becomes evident. Though there are many considerations along the road to attainment, research and personal practice is clear about the role leader influence plays. Whilst research is rich with theories that describe the attributes of successful leadership, and while these are natural and innate characteristics of some, for many it is not. As a precursor to the accomplishment of goals, I have found that it is in the application of the research that there are some gaps. It is therefore imperative that we dig deeper into the research to map out actionable plans that can be applied by the majority in paving the road forward.

In closing, be reminded of the impact and influence leaders can have on the constituents they serve. This impact or influence can be negative or positive. It is however incumbent on us to empower ourselves and those we serve with the resources necessary to ensure the latter. Leading is challenging and if done correctly there are no shortcuts to getting it right.

The information provided in this book is intended to share strategies to improve your professional practice. Grounded in theory, these strategies have proven to be practical for developing leaders to lead real people in real organizations characterized by real problems. Use them, be empowered, lead with confidence and BE UNORTHODOX!

Should you find this read enjoyable, do share or gift to empower another!
To learn more, visit:
www.unorthodoxleadership.org

REFERENCES

Anderson, J. (1983). *The architecture of cognition*. Mahwah, NJ:

Lawrence Erlbaum Associates, Inc.

Barnard, A. (2005). Help yourself. *Nursing Standard, 20*(5), 70–71.

Barnett, K., & McCormick, J. (2012). Leadership and team dynamics in senior executive leadership teams. *Educational Management Administration and Leadership, 40*(6), 653–671.

Bieri, J. (1966). Cognitive complexity and personality development. In O. Harvey (Ed.), *Experience structure and Adaptability* (pp. 13–37). New York, NY: Springer.

Bloomfield, J., Ackland, T., & Elliot, B. (1994). *Applied anatomy and biomechanics in sport*. Melbourne, VIC: Blackwell Scientific.

Boni, A., Weingart, L., & Evenson, S. (2009). Innovation in an academic setting: Designing and leading a business through market-focused, interdisciplinary teams. *Academy of Management Learning and Education, 9*(3), 407–417.

Burke, C. S., Stagl, K. C., Klein, C., Goodwin, G. F., Salas, E., & Halpin, S. M. (2006). What type of leadership behaviors are functional in teams? A meta-analysis. *The Leadership Quarterly, 17*(3), 288–307.

Cameron, K. S., Bright, D., & Caza, A. (2004). Exploring the relationships between organizational virtuousness and performance. *American Behavioral Scientist, 47*(6), 1–24.

Day, D. V., Gronn, P., & Salas, E., (2004). Leadership capacity in teams. *The Leadership Quarterly, 15*(6), 857–880.

Del Favero, M. (2006). An examination of the relationship between academic discipline and cognitive complexity in academic deans' administrative behavior. *Research in Higher Education, 47*(3), 281–315.

Denison, D., Hooijberg, R., & Quinn, R. (1995). Paradox and performance: Toward a theory of behavioral complexity in managerial leadership. *Organizational Science, 6*(5), 524–540.

Derek, A., Morfitt, G., & Demaerschalk, D. (1996). *Cognitive complexity and expertise: External and internal measures of cognitive complexity and abstraction, and responses to a case problem.* Ottawa, Canada: Social Sciences and Humanities Research Council of Canada. Retrieved from https://files.eric.ed.gov/fulltext/ED412604.pdf

Edmonson, A. (1999). Psychological safety and learning behavior in work teams. *Administrative Science Quarterly, 44*(2), 350–383.

Ernst, C. T. (2000). *The influence of behavioral complexity on global leadership effectiveness* (Doctoral dissertation). North Carolina State University, Raleigh, NC.

Evans, A. (2007). School leaders and their sense making about race and demographic change. *Educational Administration Quarterly, 43*(2), 159–188.

Falk-Krzesinski, H., Contractor, N., Fiore, S., Hall, K., Kane, C., Keyton, J.,…Trochim, W. (2011). Mapping a research agenda for the science of team science. *Research Evaluation, 20*(2), 145–158.

Gerras, S., & Clark, C. (2011, August). *Effective team leadership: A competitive advantage.* Retrieved from http://www.carlisle.army.mil/orgs/SSL/dclm/pubs/Effective Team Leadership.pdf

Gonzalez, C. (2004). Learning to make decisions in dynamic environments: Effects of time constraints and cognitive abilities. *Human Factors, 46*(3), 449–460.

Granello, D. (2010). Cognitive complexity among practicing counselors. *Journal of Counseling and Development, 88*(1), 92–100.

Granello, D., & Underfer-Babalis, J. (2004). Supervision of group work: A model to increase supervisee cognitive complexity. *Journal for Specialists in Group Work, 29*(2), 159–173.

Gulsen, C. & Gulenay, G. (2014). The principal and healthy school climate. *Social Behavior and Personality, 42*, S93–S100.

Gurr, D., & Drysdale, L. (2013). Middle-level secondary school leaders: Potential, constraints and implications for leadership preparation and development. *Journal of Educational Administration, 51*(1), 55–71.

Hackman, R. J. (2002). *Leading teams: Setting the stage for great performances*. Boston, MA: Harvard Business School Press.

Hallinger, P., Leithwood, K., & Murphy, J. (Eds.). (1993). *Cognitive perspectives on educational leadership*. New York, NY: Teachers College Press.

Hooijberg, R., (1996). A multidirectional approach toward leadership: An extension of the concept of behavioral complexity. *Human Relations, 49*(7), 917–946.

Hooijberg, R., Hunt, J., & Dodge, G. (1997). Leadership complexity and development of the leaderplex model. *Journal of Management, 23*(3), 375–408.

Hooijberg, R., & Quinn, R. E. (1992). Behavioral complexity and development of effective managers. In R. L. Phillips & J. G. Hunt (Eds.), *Strategic leadership: A multiorganizational-level perspective* (pp. 161–175). Westport: CT: Quorum.

Horney, N., Pasmore, B., & O'Shea, T. (2010). Leadership agility: A business imperative for a VUCA world. *People and Strategy, 33*(4), 32–38.

Institute for Corporate Productivity. (2010, March 11). *Agile leaders generate greater corporate performance* [Press release]. Retrieved from

http://www.pr.com/pressrelease/218637

Israel, B. A., Schulz, A. J., Parker, E. A., & Becker, A. B. (1998). Review of community-based research: Assessing partnership approaches to improve public health. *Annual Review of Public Health, 19*(1), 173–202.

Joiner, B., & Josephs, S. (2007). Leadership agility. *Leadership Excellence Essentials, 24*(6), 16.

Kaplan, R., Norton, D., & Barrows, E. (2008). Developing the strategy: Vision, value gaps, and analysis. *Balanced Scorecard Report, 10*(1), 1–5.

Katzenbach, J., & Smith, D. (1993a). The discipline of teams. *Harvard Business Review, 71*(2), 111–120.

Katzenbach, J., & Smith, D. (1993b). The wisdom of teams. *Small Business Reports, 18*(7), 68–71.

Kayes, A., Kayes, C., & Kolb, D. (2005). Experiential learning in teams. *Simulation and Gaming, 36*(3), 330–354.

Kotter, J. (1996). *Leading change.* Boston, MA: Harvard Business School Press.

Kythreotis, A., Pashiardis, P., & Kyriakides, L.(2010). The influence of school leadership styles and culture on students' achievement in Cyprus primary schools. *Journal of Educational Administration, 48*(2), 218–240.

Lawrence, K., Lenk, P., & Quinn, R. (2009). Behavioral complexity in leadership: The psychometric properties of a new instrument to measure behavioral repertoire. *The Leadership Quarterly, 20*(2), 87–102.

LePine, J. A., Colquitt, J. A., & Erez, A. (2000). Adaptability to changing task contexts: Effects of general cognitive ability, conscientiousness, and openness to experience. *Personnel Psychology, 53*(3), 563–593.

Leithwood, K. (2005). Understanding successful principal leadership: Progress on a broken front. *Journal of Educational Administration, 43*(6), 619–629.

Leithwood, K., & Mascall, B. (2008). Collective leadership effects on student achievement. *Educational Administration Quarterly, 44*(4), 529–561.

Lewis, M., Andriopoulos, C., & Wendy, S. (2014). Paradoxical leadership to enable strategic agility. *California Management Review, 56*(3), 58–77.

MacNeil, A., Prater, D., & Busch, S. (2009). The effects of school culture and climate on student achievement. *International Journal of Leadership in Education, 12*(1), 73–84.

Massingham, P. (2013). Cognitive complexity in global mindsets. *International Journal of Management, 30*(1), 232–248.

McLean, A. (2013, February 15). Distributive leadership has four key principles. *The Times Educational Supplement.* Retrieved from https://www.tes.com/news/distributive-leadership-has-four-key-principles

McKenzie, J., & Aitken, P. (2012). Learning to lead the knowledgeable organization: Developing leadership agility. *Strategic HR Review, 11*(6), 329–334.

Mumford, M. D., & Hunter, S. T. (2005). Innovation in organizations: A multi-level perspective on creativity. In F. Dansereau & F. J. Yammarino (Eds.), *Research in Multi-Level Issues, 4* (pp. 9–73). Bingley, United Kingdom: Emerald Group Publishing Limited.

Neumann, A. (1991). The thinking team: Toward a cognitive model of administrative teamwork in higher education. *The Journal of Higher Education, 62*(5), 485–513.

Nijstad, B. A., & Stroebe, W. (2006). How the group affects the mind: A cognitive model of idea generation in groups. *Personality and Social Psychology Review, 10*(3), 186–214.

O'Connor, P., & Quinn, L., (2004). Organizational capacity for leadership. In C. D. McCauley & E. Van Velsor (Eds.) *The Center for Creative Leadership Handbook of Leadership Development* (2nd ed.) (pp. 417–437). San Francisco, CA:

Jossey-Bass.

Ogilvie, K., & Jelavic, M. (2009). Multidisciplinary technical teams: A case study. *Canadian Manager, 33*(3), 18–19.

Organ, D. W., Podsakoff, P. M., & Mackenzie, S. B. (2006). *Organizational citizenship behavior: Its nature, antecedents, and consequences.* Thousand Oaks, CA: Sage Publications.

Parris, M., & Vickers, M. (2005). Working in teams: The influence of rhetoric-from sensemaking to sadness. *Administrative Theory and Praxis, 27*(2), 277–300.

Pisapia, J. (2009). *The strategic leader: New tactics for a globalizing world.* Charlotte, NC: Information Age Publishers.

Schermerhorn, J. R., Hunt, J. G., & Osborn, R. N. (2002). *Organizational behavior.* New York, NY: Wiley.

Sheppard, J., & Young, W. (2006). Agility literature review: Classifications, training and testing. *Journal of Sports Science, 24*(9), 919–932.

Spillane, J., Diamond, J., Burch, P., Hallett, T., Jita, L., & Zoltners, J.

(2002). Managing in the middle: School leaders and the enactment of accountability policy. *Educational Policy, 16*(5), 731–762.

Stokols, D., Misra, S., Moser, R., Hall, K., & Taylor, B. (2008). The ecology of team science: Understanding contextual influences on transdisciplinary collaboration. *American Journal of Preventive Medicine, 35*(2), 96–115.

Thornton, R. (2005). Tactical agility: Linking the cognitive and physical using networked battle command. *Armor, 114*(6), 35–40.

Tsui, A. S. (1984). A role set analysis of managerial reputation. *Organizational Behavior and Human Performance, 34*(1), 64–96.

Weick, K. E. (1995). *Sensemaking in organizations.* Thousand Oaks, CA: Sage Publications.

Wendt, H., Euwema, M., & van Emmerik, H. (2009). Leadership and team cohesiveness across cultures. *The Leadership Quarterly, 20*(3), 358–370.

Williams, D. (1994). *Leadership in the 21st century: Life insurance leadership study.* Boston, MA: Hay Group.

Zaccaro, S. J. (2001). *The nature of executive leadership: A conceptual and empirical analysis of success.* Washington, DC: American Psychological Association.